the TREE in the ANCIENT FOREST

To the children of Bayside Montessori School — for
their enthusiasm! — *Carol Reed-Jones*

This book is dedicated to Angel, Nicolas, Michelle,
Elise, my brother Kelly, and my loving
wife Jeanette. — *Christopher Canyon*

Library of Congress Cataloging-in-Publication Data
Reed-Jones, Carol.
The tree in the ancient forest / Carol Reed-Jones ;
illustrations by Christopher Canyon. — 1st ed. — Nevada City, CA :
Dawn Publications, c1995.
1 v. (unpaged) : col. ill. ; 31 cm.
SUMMARY: "The remarkable web of plants and animals living around a single old
fir tree takes on a life of its own." in this story about "the amazing ways in which
the [forest] inhabitants depend upon one another for survival."
Audience: "Ages 4-10."
ISBN 1-88322-032-7 (hardback)
ISBN 1-88322-031-9 (paperback)
1. Forest fauna—Juvenile literature. 2. Forest plants—Juvenile literature.
I. Canyon, Christopher, ill. II. Title.
QL83.R44 1995 591.52'642 QBI95-20329

Published by Dawn Publications
12402 Bitney Springs Road
Nevada City, CA 95959
800-545-7475
nature@DawnPub.com

Manufactured by Regent Publishing Services, Hong Kong
Printed June, 2017 in Shenzhen, Guangdong, China

15

Designed by LeeAnn Brook
Type style is Stone Serif
Illustrations are done in acrylic paint with
a textured gesso underlay.

the TREE in the ANCIENT FOREST

Carol Reed-Jones
Illustrations by Christopher Canyon

DAWN Publications

In all of nature, there is something of the wonderful.

—Aristotle

Truly there is something wonderful in every bit of nature. Every animal and plant, no matter how small—even if it is microscopic—is important in nature. The plants and animals in this story depend upon one another for survival. This kind of mutual need is called **interdependence**.

Somewhere near your home is a wild, natural area where the plants and animals all rely upon one another. It may be a woodland or a wetland, a prairie, desert, jungle or tundra. Even if the plants and animals living near you are different from those in this story, they all are interdependent in the same kinds of ways that the plants and animals in this story are.

Walk softly when you go to a wild place. If you must speak, whisper. Look for the birds, insects and other animals that live there. Sit in one place for a few minutes without speaking or moving. Listen to the many different sounds. Which sounds are made by birds? How many of them are made by insects or larger animals? Can you smell flowers, other plants—even the soil? Is there a breeze that makes grass, leaves, or branches rustle? Do you hear water from a stream? Look closely at the ground. What tiny insects and plants can you find? You will probably find many more living things than you first imagined!

Just as all of these plants and animals depend upon one another, we also depend upon all of nature. It is important that we learn to preserve and respect these living things, not only for ourselves, but for our children and grandchildren and all the wonderful creatures who share this planet with us.

This is the ancient forest.

This is the three-hundred-year-old tree
That grows in the ancient forest.

These are the roots that draw food from the soil
To nourish the three-hundred-year-old tree
That grows in the ancient forest.

These are the tiny, underground truffles
That grow on roots that draw food from the soil,
To nourish the three-hundred-year-old tree
That grows in the ancient forest.

These are the voles and mice that tunnel,
And eat the tiny, underground truffles
That grow on roots that draw food from the soil,
To nourish the three-hundred-year-old tree
That grows in the ancient forest.

This is the owl that flies at night
That hunts the voles and mice that tunnel
And eat the tiny, underground truffle
That grow on roots that draw food from the soil
To nourish the three-hundred-year-old tre
That grows in the ancient forest

These are the sleepy owlets,
That are fed by the owl that flies at night,
That hunts the voles and mice that tunnel,
And eat the tiny, underground truffles
That grow on roots that draw food from the soil,
To nourish the three-hundred-year-old tree
That grows in the ancient forest.

This is a hollow in the tree,
Home of the sleepy owlets,
That are fed by the owl that flies at night,
That hunts the voles and mice that tunnel,
And eat the tiny, underground truffles
That grow on roots that draw food from the soil,
To nourish the three-hundred-year-old tree
That grows in the ancient forest.

This is the woodpecker,
searching for ants,
That started the hollow
in the tree,
Home of the sleepy owlets,
That are fed by the owl
that flies at night,
That hunts the voles and
mice that tunnel,
And eat the tiny
underground truffles
That grow on roots
that draw food
from the soil,
To nourish the
three-hundred-year-old tree
That grows in the
ancient forest.

This is the saucy, chattering squirrel
That scolds the woodpecker, searching for ants,
That started the hollow in the tree,
Home of the sleepy owlets,
That are fed by the owl that flies at night,
That hunts the voles and mice that tunnel,
And eat the tiny, underground truffles
That grow on roots that draw food from the soil,
To nourish the three-hundred-year-old tree
That grows in the ancient forest.

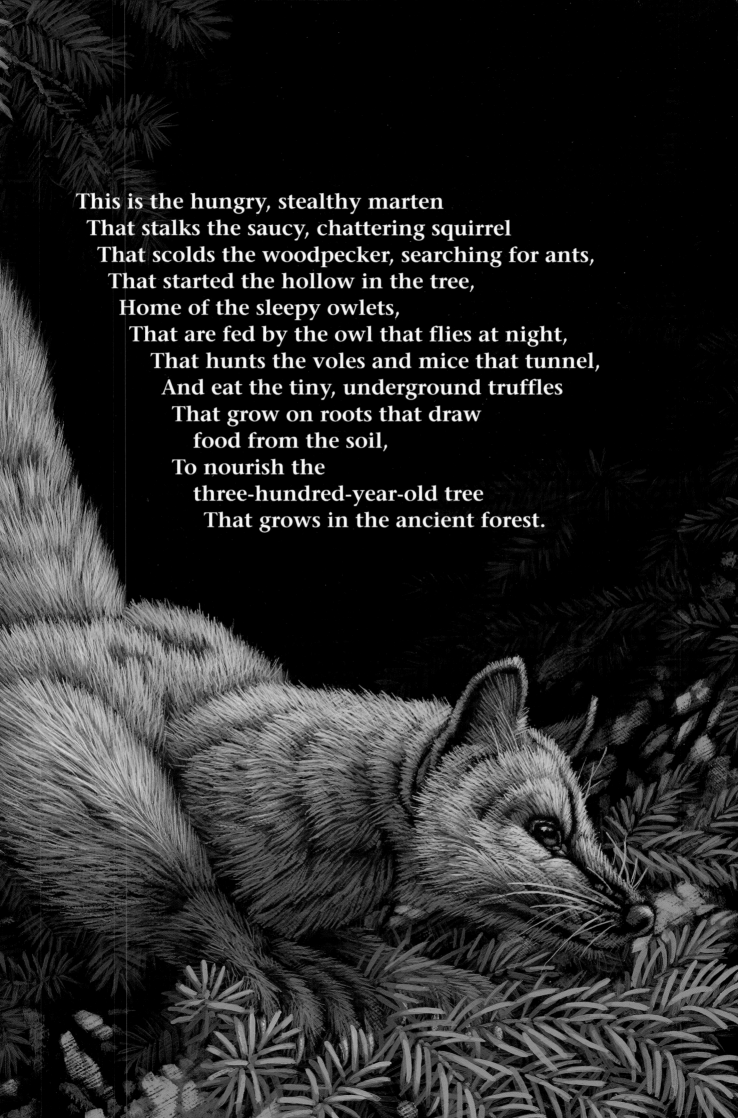

This is the hungry, stealthy marten
That stalks the saucy, chattering squirrel
That scolds the woodpecker, searching for ants,
That started the hollow in the tree,
Home of the sleepy owlets,
That are fed by the owl that flies at night,
That hunts the voles and mice that tunnel,
And eat the tiny, underground truffles
That grow on roots that draw
food from the soil,
To nourish the
three-hundred-year-old tree
That grows in the ancient forest.

These are the fir cones that fall from a branch,
And startle the hungry, stealthy marten
That stalks the saucy, chattering squirrel
That scolds the woodpecker, searching for ants,
That started the hollow in the tree,
Home of the sleepy owlets,
That are fed by the owl that flies at night,
That hunts the voles and mice that tunnel,
And eat the tiny underground truffles
That grow on roots that draw food from the soil,
To nourish the three-hundred-year-old tree
That grows in the ancient forest.

This is the three-hundred-year-old tree,
That grows the fir cones that
   fall from a branch,
And startle the hungry, stealthy marten
That stalks the saucy, chattering squirrel
That scolds the woodpecker, searching for ants,
That started the hollow in the tree,
Home of the sleepy owlets,
That are fed by the owl that flies at night,
   That hunts the voles and mice that tunnel,
      And eat the tiny, underground truffles
         That grow on roots that draw
            food from the soil,
         To nourish the
            three-hundred-year-old tree
               That grows in the ancient forest.

The Characters In This Story

Only a few of the plants and animals in an ancient forest were chosen to be characters in this story. There are many, many more. All are interdependent in some way, and each one plays an important role in the health of the forest.

A **DOUGLAS FIR TREE** can be as old as 1000 years, and as tall as 300 feet. It is home to voles, owls, martens, Douglas squirrels and flying squirrels. Birds and rodents eat the seeds in the cones, deer eat the new shoots, and black bears sometimes eat the sap layer under the bark.

The **ROOTS** are very shallow for such a tall tree. Most of the roots lie just 3 feet underground, but spread out from the trunk for many yards.

TRUFFLES are only 3/8 to 2 inches in diameter. They are the underground fruits of mycorrhizae *(my-co-RYE-zay)*. Mycorrhizae are fungi that attach themselves to tree root tips, or enter the roots themselves, and help the roots use nutrients from the soil. The roots help the mycorrhizae absorb nutrients, too. Truffles and tree roots are so necessary to one another that trees without truffles may die. This partnership is a good example of interdependence.

VOLES AND MICE eat truffles year-round except in winter. When they eat the truffles, the truffle spores (seeds) are not harmed. Truffle spores in the rodents' droppings are then deposited on the forest floor, and grow into more truffles. Every time a mouse or vole eats a truffle, it is helping to plant more truffles.

NORTHERN SPOTTED OWLS eat voles, mice, and flying squirrels. Spotted owls are very trusting, and are curious about humans. Other owls that live in the ancient forest are the great horned owl, barred owl, saw whet owl, pygmy owl and western screech owl. The spotted owl is an endangered species—it could become extinct.

Two, or sometimes three, **OWLETS** are born to a pair of spotted owls every other year. They nest only in ancient forests.

The nest **HOLLOW** was created by a lightning wound to the tree. The tree formed a fire scar, which attracted a wood-boring beetle. Carpenter ants moved in to eat the dead wood, and woodpeckers dug for insects. Spotted owls also nest on platforms created by mistletoe, or formed when a storm breaks the crown or top of a tree.

A **PILEATED WOODPECKER** helped make the hollow by digging for insects that eat dead wood. These woodpeckers dig their own nest cavities. If the woodpeckers move out, other animals may move in: Douglas squirrels, flying squirrels, martens, bats, tree swallows, or the Western screech owl.

DOUGLAS SQUIRRELS eat truffles and Douglas fir seeds during the day. Another squirrel in the ancient forest is the flying squirrel, which also eats truffles and is active at night. Flying squirrels don't actually fly, but they do jump and glide through the air by using skin flaps along their sides, between their front and back feet.

The **MARTEN** is a shy relative of the weasel. Martens live mostly up in the trees, and are not often seen by humans. They eat squirrels, rabbits, mice, birds, eggs, berries, seeds from cone-bearing trees, and even sometimes honey.

The **CONES** from Douglas fir trees have seeds that many animals eat. The seeds are very light; 42,000 seeds weigh only one pound. Vast numbers of them fall from the cones and drift up to one-quarter of a mile from their parent tree in a moderate breeze, spinning and twirling because of small tear-shaped "wings" on each seed. Each of these seeds has within it the living code that will shape the future forest.

What Is An Ancient Forest?

An ancient forest is a natural forest that has been allowed to grow undisturbed for at least 200 years. The trees in an ancient forest may be as old as 1000 years, or even older. The ancient forest in this story is in the Pacific Northwest, but its main characteristics are shared by ancient forests the world over. Ancient forests have:

Large, OLD STANDING TREES, which shelter or feed nearly all the animals in the forest.

Standing dead trees, called SNAGS, which are homes to many animals—insects, woodpeckers, swifts, bats, owls, martens, squirrels and others.

FALLEN TREES, which provide shelter for animals, food for insects and other animals, and release nutrients into the soil when they decay. Fallen trees collect mosses and lichen, and *duff,* decaying leaves and other organic matter. This material creates a rich soil for tree seedlings and other plants. A decaying fallen tree with younger trees growing on top of it is called a *nurse tree.*

A MULTI-STORIED, MULTI-SPECIES FOREST CANOPY. This means that the forest's "roof" has many different levels, with many different sizes, ages and species of trees. There are natural patches of shade and sunlight on the forest floor. By contrast, commercial stands of timber are mostly uniform in species and age, and are rarely over 100 years old.

Why Are Ancient Forests Important?

Ancient forests are critical to animals—and to us. Of the animals in this story, the marten, pileated woodpecker and northern spotted owl are especially dependent upon very large old trees. If they do not have ancient forests in which to live, they may become extinct. In addition, we are only now beginning to discover plants and animals that are unique to ancient forests. They may be helpful to us in ways that we do not yet understand.

Ancient forests purify the air. A single old-growth Douglas fir tree can have as many as 60 million needles, with a total surface area of about 1 acre. These needles are constantly filtering the air, absorbing carbon dioxide and producing life-giving oxygen. An excess of carbon dioxide is considered to be mainly responsible for global warming (the "greenhouse effect").

Ancient forests are irreplaceable. It takes a forest at least 200 years of undisturbed growth even to *begin* to have the characteristics that make it an ancient forest. Cutting down an ancient forest is not like mowing a lawn. Once an ancient forest is cut, we will never see it again.

Even though over 90 percent of the ancient forests in North America have been cut, we can still save the remaining 10 percent. We can use wood products wisely, purchasing wood that has not been cut from ancient forests. We can use recycled paper, or paper from other vegetable fibers such as cotton. And we can support laws that will protect these forests.

About the Author

Carol Reed-Jones lives in the Pacific Northwest where she loves to walk in ancient forests. She used the literary style of cumulative verse, as in "This is the house that Jack built," to portray the interdependence of the forest and its animals. As a music teacher she pays attention to the rhythm and the cadence of the words. Carol also loves to watch salmon in the rivers and streams, and wrote *Salmon Stream* (published by Dawn Publications) about the life cycle of those remarkable migrating fish.

About the Illustrator

Christopher Canyon is irrepressibly playful as well as passionate about illustrating children's books. He is a musician and performer dedicated to sharing the joy and importance of the arts with children, educators, and families. He and his wife, Jeanette Canyon — also a picture book illustrator — frequently visit schools, providing educational and entertaining programs. Christopher has illustrated numerous books for Dawn Publications, including *Stickeen: John Muir and the Brave Little Dog*. He also adapted and illustrated four of John Denver's songs as picture books in the "John Denver & Kids" series from Dawn Publications.

OTHER NATURE AWARENESS BOOKS FROM DAWN PUBLICATIONS

Nature's Patchwork Quilt: Understanding Habitats, by Mary Miché, illustrated by Consie Powell. Nature's many habitats fit together beautifully, just like a patchwork quilt — and each habitat illustrates a key scientific concept.

In the Trees, Honey Bees, by Lori Mortensen, illustrated by Cris Arbo — a remarkable inside-the-hive view of a wild colony of honeybees, along with simple rhymes and solid information. A favorite among young bee-lovers.

Salmon Stream, by Carol Reed-Jones, illustrated by Michael Maydak, follows the life cycle of salmon that hatch in a stream, travel the oceans, and return to their birthplace against staggering odds.

Stickeen: John Muir and the Brave Little Dog, by Donnell Rubay, illustrated by Christopher Canyon. In this classic true story, the relationship between the great naturalist and a small dog is changed forever by their adventure on a glacier in Alaska.

The award-winning **HABITAT SERIES** by Anthony Fredericks, illustrated by Jennifer DiRubbio, features creature-communities, seen as part of their own unique neighborhood: *Around One Log, Under One Rock; In One Tidepool; Around One Cactus; Near One Cattail* and *On One Flower.*

Dawn Publications is dedicated to inspiring in children a deeper understanding and appreciation for all life on Earth. To order, or for a copy of our catalog, please call 800-545-7475. Please also visit our web site at www.dawnpub.com.